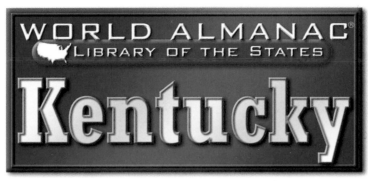

THE BLUEGRASS STATE

by Miriam Heddy Pollock and Peter Jaffe

Curriculum Consultant: Jean Craven,
Director of Instructional Support,
Albuquerque, NM, Public Schools

WORLD ALMANAC® LIBRARY

Please visit our web site at: **www.worldalmaclibrary.com**
For a free color catalog describing World Almanac® Library's
list of high-quality books and multimedia programs, call
1-800-848-2928 (USA) or 1-800-387-3178 (Canada).
World Almanac® Library's fax: (414) 332-3567.

Library of Congress Cataloging-in-Publication Data

Pollock, Miriam Heddy.
    Kentucky, the Bluegrass State / by Miriam Heddy Pollock and Peter Jaffe.
       p. cm. — (World Almanac Library of the states)
    Includes bibliographical references and index.
    Summary: Presents the history, geography, people, politics and government, economy,
social life and customs, state events and attractions, and notable people of Kentucky.
    ISBN 0-8368-5135-8 (lib. bdg.)
    ISBN 0-8368-5305-9 (softcover)
    1. Kentucky—Juvenile literature. [1. Kentucky.] I. Title. II. Jaffe, Peter.
III. Series.
F451.3.I54   2002
976.9—dc21   2002069121

This edition first published in 2002 by
World Almanac® Library
330 West Olive Street, Suite 100
Milwaukee, WI 53212 USA

This edition © 2002 by World Almanac® Library.

Design and Editorial: Bill SMITH STUDIO Inc.
Editor: Kristen Behrens
Assistant Editor: Megan Elias
Art Director: Olga Lamm
Photo Research: Sean Livingstone
World Almanac® Library Project Editor: Patricia Lantier
World Almanac® Library Editors: Monica Rausch, Mary Dykstra, Catherine Gardner
World Almanac® Library Production: Scott M. Krall, Tammy Gruenewald,
  Katherine A. Goedheer

Photo credits: pp. 4-5 © PhotoDisc; p. 6 (all) © Corel; p. 7 (top) © PhotoSpin, (bottom) © Corel;
p. 9 Courtesy of the Library of Congress; p. 10 © ArtToday; p. 11 © Dover; p. 12 © CORBIS; p. 13
Courtesy of the Library of Congress; p. 14 © Ed Clark/CORBIS; p. 15 © Kentucky Department
of Libraries and Archives; p. 17 Courtesy of the Library of Congress; p. 18 © PhotoDisc; p. 19
© James Burke/TimePix; p. 20 (left to right) © Kentucky Dept. of Travel Development, © Lexington
CVB, © Lexington CVB; p. 21 (left to right) © ArtToday, © Lexington CVB, © PhotoDisc; p. 23
© Kentucky Dept. of Travel Development; p. 26 (top) courtesy of Toyota, (bottom) © PhotoDisc;
p. 27 (all) © PhotoDisc; p. 29 © Kentucky Tourism; p. 30 Courtesy of the Library of Congress; p. 31
Courtesy of the Library of Congress; p. 33 © Corel; p. 34 © Thomas S. England/TimePix; p. 35 ©
Lexington CVB; p. 36 (top) © Shaker Village of Pleasant Hill, (bottom) © Tom G. Lynn/TimePix; p. 37
© Lexington CVB; p. 38 © Dover; p. 39 © ArtToday; p. 40 (all) © Dover; p. 41 (all) © Dover;
pp. 42-43 Courtesy of the Library of Congress; p. 44 (all) © PhotoDisc; p. 45 © Corel

Printed in the United States of America

1 2 3 4 5 6 7 8 9 06 05 04 03 02

Kentucky

Diverse Beauty

T he Bluegrass State is a land of mountains and prairies, of floodplains and coal fields, all of which have contributed to the character of the state. The diversity of the landscape is echoed in the diversity of the residents. The people of the Appalachian Mountains, the coal miners of the central hills, the horse breeders of the prairies, the industrialists of the big cities, and the tobacco farmers in the west are all Kentuckians. They form so many different communities that it is impossible to say which is "typical."

Although diversity is one of the state's great strengths, it also has led to hardship. During the Civil War, Kentucky was torn between loyalties to the Union and to the Confederacy. Kentucky was a slaveholding state but also had strong abolitionist tendencies and refused to secede. On the border between North and South, it has never fully identified with either region, a testament to the wide range of beliefs Kentuckians hold.

Kentucky has always depended on its natural resources. Again, this dependence has served as both a boon and a burden. The abundant forests that covered the eastern part of the state were a ready source of lumber for the early pioneers. The eventual overharvesting of the woodlands, however, led to deforestation and a loss of ecological diversity. The advent of coal mining meant a huge economic boost and provided steady employment for thousands of people for many years. Over time, however, the exploitation of this environmentally harmful resource led to pollution and health problems. The economic benefits disappeared, too, as the nation began switching to cleaner forms of fuel, and coal miners fell on hard times.

The people of Kentucky, however, have always shown resilience and an ability to adapt that has positioned the state well for the new century.

▶ Map of Kentucky showing the interstate highway system, as well as major cities and waterways.

▼ The former Winchester plantation in eastern Kentucky is today a horse farm.

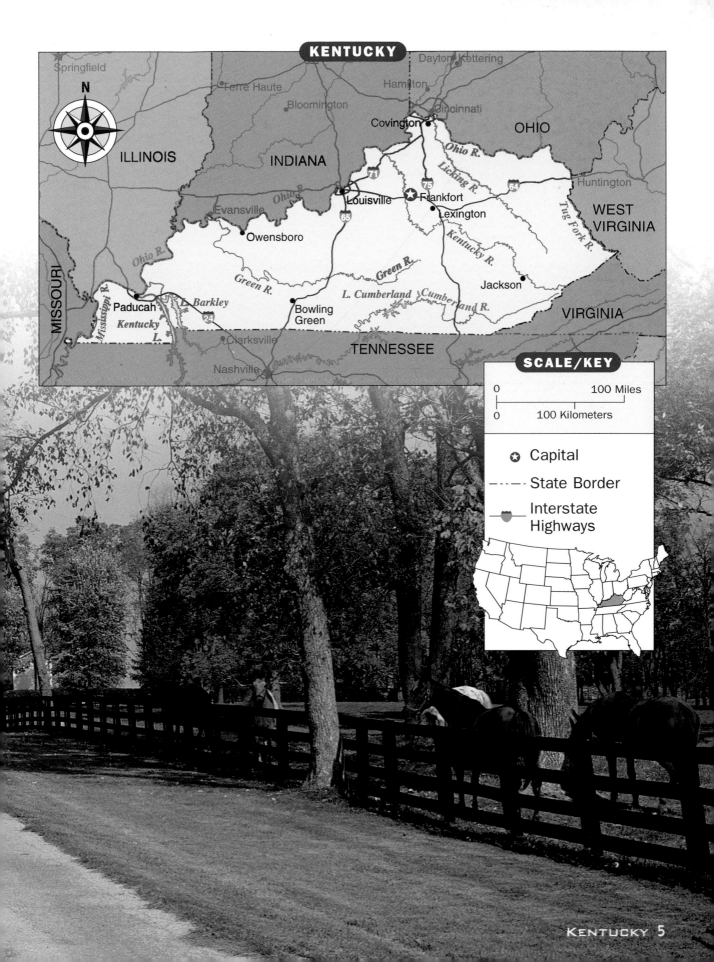

KENTUCKY

Springfield
Terre Haute
Bloomington
Dayton Kettering
Hamilton
Cincinnati
Covington
OHIO
Ohio R.
Licking R.
Huntington
Louisville
Frankfort
Lexington
WEST VIRGINIA
Tug Fork R.
ILLINOIS
INDIANA
Evansville
Ohio R.
Owensboro
Kentucky R.
Ohio R.
Green R.
Green R.
Jackson
MISSOURI
Mississippi R.
L. Barkley
L. Cumberland
Cumberland R.
VIRGINIA
Paducah
Kentucky L.
Bowling Green
Clarksville
TENNESSEE
Nashville

SCALE/KEY

0   100 Miles
0   100 Kilometers

⭐ Capital
---·--- State Border
Interstate Highways

Fast Facts

Kentucky (KY), The Bluegrass State

Entered Union

June 1, 1792 (15th state)

Capital	Population
Frankfort	.27,741

Total Population (2000)

4,041,769 (25th most populous state)
*Between 1990 and 2000 the
population of Kentucky increased
9.7 percent.*

Largest Cities	Population
Lexington	260,512
Louisville	256,231
Owensboro	54,067
Bowling Green	49,296
Covington	43,370

Land Area

39,728 square miles
(102,896 square kilometers)
(36th largest state)

State Motto

"United We Stand, Divided
We Fall"

State Song

"My Old Kentucky Home" *by Stephen
C. Foster, modern version adopted
in 1986.*

State Bluegrass Song

"Blue Moon of Kentucky," *by
Bill Monroe, adopted in 1988.*

State Wild Animal

Gray squirrel

State Bird

Cardinal

State Fish

Kentucky bass

State Butterfly

Viceroy — *Its similarity
in appearance to the
orange-and-black
monarch butterfly protects the
viceroy from being eaten by birds.
The monarch is poisonous so birds
avoid both monarchs and the
look-alike viceroys.*

State Tree

Tulip tree

State Flower

Goldenrod

State Fossil

Brachiopod — *A brachiopod
was a bivalve, or two-shelled,
mollusk that lived on the ocean
floor. Brachiopod fossils are
probably the most common fossils
found in Kentucky, suggesting that
this area was once at the bottom
of an ocean.*

State Gemstone

Freshwater pearl — *Kentucky
freshwater pearls come from mussels
rather than from oysters and clams.*

State Horse

Thoroughbred

PLACES TO VISIT

Mammoth Cave National Park, *Mammoth Cave*
In addition to being the largest known cave system in the world, Mammoth Cave is also home to more than two hundred species of animals, including troglobites — animals that live out their entire lives in the dark. This national park also offers hiking, camping, and horseback riding, as well as spelunking, or exploring caves.

Fort Boonesborough State Park, *near Richmond*
Boonesborough, established by Daniel Boone in 1775, became a fort and trade center. Today visitors can see costumed interpreters reenact the fort's founding as well as the lifestyles of Kentucky's earliest non-Native inhabitants.

Kentucky Horse Park, *near Lexington*
This 1,200-acre (486-hectare) park is home to more than two hundred horses representing about fifty breeds. Visitors can learn about the history of the horse, watch a blacksmith at work, or take a carriage ride or trail ride.

For other places and events, see p. 44.

BIGGEST, BEST, AND MOST

- The Kentucky Derby is the nation's oldest continuously held horse race.
- The Cathedral Basilica of the Assumption in Covington is reputed to have the largest hand-blown stained glass church window in the world.

STATE FIRSTS

- **1792** Kentucky becomes the first state west of the Appalachians.
- **1853** Kentucky-born William Wells Brown publishes *Clotel*, the first novel published by an African American.
- **1949** At seventy-one, Alben W. Barkley becomes the oldest man to become a U.S. vice president.

Happy Birthday from Kentucky

In 1893, two sisters in Louisville composed a song that would become one of the most popular songs in the English language. Mildred Hill was a kindergarten teacher and Patty a school principal when Mildred composed music for the tune that would become famous as "Happy Birthday to You." Patty wrote lyrics to accompany the music — "Good morning dear teacher, good morning to you." For decades, this song was used to start off the day in many schools around the nation. In the early 1930s new words were added, making it a birthday song. In 1933 the song was used in the musical *As Thousands Cheer* and became a national hit. The song remains under copyright and earns more than $1 million each year for the music company that owns the rights to it.

Little Red Corvette

The idea of the Chevrolet Corvette was born in 1951 when General Motors's chief stylist, Harley Earl, attended a sports car race where European automobiles inspired him to design a new U.S. sports car. In 1952, the prototype was approved and the new car was named. Although initially a marketing failure, the 1956 model began to break records at raceways, and the car finally became a success. Today all Corvettes are manufactured in Bowling Green.

From Frontier to Coal Fields

> . . . [W]e view Kentucky situated on the fertile banks of the great Ohio, rising from obscurity to shine with splendor, equal to any other of the states of the American hemisphere.
>
> — *Daniel Boone, frontiersman*

Humans lived in the area now known as Kentucky as long as fourteen thousand years ago. Artifacts such as spear tips suggest that they moved through the region while hunting large animals such as mastodons.

About three thousand years ago, agricultural societies began to develop. The Adena were Mound Builders who occupied the Ohio River Valley, which extends into Kentucky. The Adena erected burial mounds up to 300 feet (91 meters) in diameter to inter the bodies of their most important people.

About one thousand years ago, the Mississippian people built permanent settlements in the region. When the first European settlers arrived, however, there were few Native Americans living in the region. Archaeologists are uncertain as to why they left the area.

Of those who remained, the Cherokee and Chickasaw had a minor presence. The Shawnee, Delaware, Iroquois, and Wyandot hunted in parts of Kentucky.

Gateway to the West

European settlement of the region was initially slow because the Cumberland and Pine Mountains were difficult to cross, and also because the Shawnee and Cherokee opposed attempts by newcomers to settle. Daniel Boone made several trips to Kentucky in the mid-1700s. He helped to open the Wilderness Road, which became the main thoroughfare for settlers on their way west and encouraged the settlement of Kentucky.

In 1775, the Transylvania Company was formed to colonize lands west of the mountains, which had been purchased from the Cherokee. Daniel Boone worked for the company and helped found Fort Boonesborough, southeast

Native Americans of Kentucky
Adena
Cherokee
Chickasaw
Delaware
Iroquois
Mississippian
Shawnee
Wyandot

DID YOU KNOW?

The name "Kentucky" comes from a Native American word, although which word — and what it means — is subject to debate. It may come from the Cherokee word *ken-ta-ten*, meaning "land of tomorrow"; from the Iroquois name for the Shawnee town of Eskippathiki; or from a Wyandot word meaning "plain," referring to the state's central plains.

of present-day Lexington. During the Revolutionary War the fort was attacked numerous times by Native Americans, who were encouraged to do so by the British. In 1778, the Virginia Legislature declared the company's purchase of Cherokee lands void, and most land in the Kentucky region became counties under Virginia's control.

After the Revolutionary War, settlers poured into the region. In the early 1780s, Kentuckians began holding statehood conventions. Ten were held in all, and in 1789 the Virginia Legislature voted to allow the Kentucky counties to become a separate state. On June 1, 1792, the Commonwealth of Kentucky was admitted to the Union as the fifteenth state.

The Nineteenth Century

Kentucky grew rapidly in the early 1800s. The increased use of steamboats, the building of canals, and the construction of railroad lines that linked Lexington and Frankfort, and later Lexington and Nashville, Tennessee, gave farmers access to more markets for their crops. Among the crops they sold were hemp for making rope, tobacco, and grains for making alcoholic beverages.

Tobacco and hemp cultivation depended on slave labor, which at that time was legal in Kentucky. Factory owners and small farmers opposed slavery because they believed it gave slave owners an unfair advantage. Factory owners had to pay their workers, and small farmers who could not afford slaves had to compete with owners of large plantations. Other Kentuckians opposed slavery on moral grounds. The state, therefore, was home to abolitionists; to people who were ardently pro-slavery; and to Free Soilers, who opposed the extension of slavery into new U.S. territories.

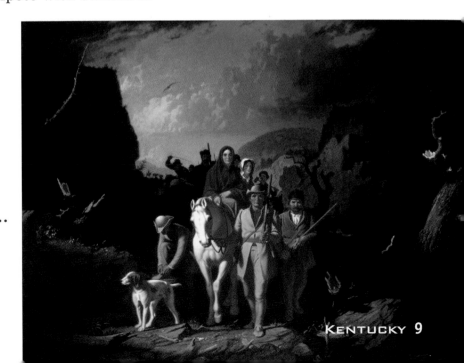

▶ This view of Daniel Boone leading settlers through the Cumberland Gap was painted in 1851-52 by George Caleb Bingham.

Battle of Perryville, Ky., from a sketch by H. Mosler in *Harper's Weekly*, Nov. 1, 1862

The Battle of Perryville

In August 1862, the Confederacy captured Lexington and Frankfort, nearly gaining control of the state, but these gains quickly slipped away. The Union army was growing as new volunteers from Louisville and elsewhere joined to push the invading Confederate army back. As the Union army gained force, it moved eastward across the state, making a showdown inevitable.

The two forces met on October 8. The Confederates nearly broke through the Union line to flank the Union forces, despite being greatly outnumbered. In the end, however, the greater numbers proved too much to overcome, and the Confederate army retreated. More than seven thousand men were killed or injured. One of the fiercest Civil War battles on Kentucky soil, the Battle of Perryville marked the end of the Confederate presence in the state.

Between North and South

As Southern states began to secede from the Union in 1861, debate raged in Kentucky. The governor, Beriah Magoffin, thought the state had the right to secede. He hoped, however, that a war between the states could be avoided. Meanwhile the state legislature tended to support the Northern states, opposing secession. When war broke out Kentucky declared itself neutral, even though this neutrality was not peaceful — the state was in chaos.

From the outset Kentuckians volunteered for both sides. As many as ninety thousand Kentuckians served in the Union army, while about forty thousand fought on the Confederate side. Union troops were recruited mainly from the northern part of the state. U.S. Army bases were established in Ohio and Indiana, along the Kentucky border.

Most whites in the state's southern region had Confederate sympathies. The Confederacy built forts just across the border in Tennessee, allowing for the easy recruitment of troops. The State Guard, or Kentucky militia, was a volunteer army organized by the legislature, but it tended to favor the Confederacy and many crossed over from Tennessee to join it.

By autumn of 1861, the state's neutrality was tested as both the Union and the Confederacy began capturing towns. Not allied with either side, Kentucky was caught in the middle and became a battleground on which the opposing armies fought.

Pro-Union James F. Robinson became governor in 1862 when Beriah Magoffin resigned. Later that same year the Confederacy installed a governor of its own, Richard Hawes, in Confederate-held Frankfort. Although the

Union more or less succeeded in gaining control of the state, its armies immediately moved on to battles in other places. Kentucky was left, again, in a state of chaos.

For the remainder of the war, bands of guerrillas raided towns throughout the state. In 1861, the Kentucky Home Guard, a Union militia, was formed to replace the State Guard troops. It was responsible for defending towns from raiders. In many cases, however, the Home Guard was merely looking for excuses to fight, further contributing to the chaotic situation.

Reconstruction

When the war ended, the U.S. government tried to reestablish order throughout the South in a process known as Reconstruction. Reconstruction was also intended to secure civil rights for African Americans. Beginning in 1865, the federal government applied many Reconstruction programs to Kentucky because it had been a slaveholding state, although not a member of the Confederacy.

Many Kentuckians felt that the U.S. government policies were heavy-handed and that Kentucky was being treated as if it were a conquered enemy. When the federal government freed all the slaves, former slave owners were angry because they were not offered payment for what they considered lost property. Many white Kentuckians were also angry at the length of time that federal troops remained in the state and because some of these troops were African-American.

Kentuckians began to identify with the South, even though a majority of residents had supported the North during the war. Conservatives who opposed the federal government were elected to the state government, and for years the Kentucky legislature concentrated on undoing the laws that had been imposed during Reconstruction. Although no longer held in slavery, many African Americans left Kentucky after the war, moving north in search of better work opportunities and a less segregated, more tolerant society.

The state also suffered from an economic depression that affected most of the South at this time. Louisville was Kentucky's only large city, and there was little industry in the state. Most of the people were farmers living in and around small towns. Much of the population was isolated because there were few public roads that would allow travel

▲ Both Jefferson Davis (*above*), the president of the Confederacy, and Abraham Lincoln, president of the United States during the Civil War, were born in Kentucky.

DID YOU KNOW?

Approximately twenty-four thousand African-American men from Kentucky enlisted in the Union army. Most were employed as guards at camps throughout the state, but some saw action in battles in Tennessee, Virginia, and North Carolina.

within the state. The construction of additional railroads was delayed due to a dispute between industrial Louisville and agricultural central Kentucky over who would control valuable routes. These factors hampered the development of Kentucky's postwar economy.

When new railroads finally were built, they helped make Louisville, which was also a port along the Ohio River, a central trading point between the North and South. Tobacco remained important to the state's economy.

Coal Mining Times

The new rail links played a part in the most significant development in the state's economy — coal mining. In 1870, Kentucky produced 150,000 tons of coal. By 1880, production was up to 1,000,000 tons per year. With the boost to the state's economy, however, came a new set of problems.

Industrialization displaced old lifestyles. Those who traditionally had supported themselves through agriculture became coal miners to gain a steady source of income. They soon discovered that coal mines produced wealth but that the financial benefits did not filter down to the miners. Many who had attempted to escape the poverty of subsistence farming or joblessness now found themselves dependent on the mining companies. Workers began

Another Civil War

Throughout the late 1800s, feuds developed between some families within small Appalachian Mountain farming communities. Sometimes feuds occurred because neighbors had supported different sides in the Civil War. The most famous of these feuds involved the Hatfield family, whose members lived mainly in West Virginia, and a Kentucky family, the McCoys. One of the earliest known conflicts occurred in 1878, when Randolph McCoy accused Floyd Hatfield of stealing a razorback hog. The feud lasted about ten years and resulted in the deaths of at least ten men. It was not, however, the longest or bloodiest of the feuds in Kentucky history. The Rowan County War, which raged in the mid-1880s, reduced the population of a local town by eight hundred people, a decline caused partly by people who moved away to escape local violence.

◀ A portrait of the Hatfield family men, taken in the 1880s. The feud between the Hatfields and the McCoys shook parts of Kentucky and West Virginia in the late nineteenth century.

forming unions, demanding that miners be paid fair wages and work under reasonable conditions.

The Black Patch War

In the first decade of the 1900s, a battle took place in Kentucky's southwestern Black Patch region, so named because dark tobacco grew best there. Farmers rebelled against the large tobacco-buying companies, which had worked together to fix prices and control markets. The farmers formed a growers' association in an attempt to oppose the companies' power. At night, however, some of these farmers became night riders, who burned the warehouses and fields of both buyers and farmers who would not join the association. Eventually, in 1908, the two sides reached an agreement that limited the buyers' monopoly.

▲ Kentucky children wait in a food line during the Great Depression. The aid being offered here was provided by the Quakers, Society of Friends, a religious group.

World War I and the Great Depression

The outbreak of World War I brought economic benefits to Kentucky. Coal production increased, bringing prosperity to the mining industry. Agricultural and business interests also prospered during the war.

The boom times did not last long, however. Economic recovery continued after the war ended in 1918 but soon began to falter. Even before the Great Depression hit, Kentucky's farmers were among the poorest in the nation.

The U.S. economy crashed in 1929, and Kentucky suffered along with the rest of the nation. Then the New Deal, a federal program designed to combat the effects of the Great Depression by creating jobs and investing in public works, brought a number of improvements to the state. Schools were renovated, and new ones built; roads were constructed, connecting even the most rural sections of the state; and telephone lines were installed statewide. The construction of the Kentucky Dam brought jobs and electricity to people throughout southwestern Kentucky.

World War II and the Modern Era

During World War II, industrialization intensified in Kentucky as the state took part in the mobilization for the war. Although Kentucky farms helped to feed U.S. soldiers

"Sixteen Tons"

Mining companies established towns such as Lynch, Jenkins, and Colmar, where workers lived in houses owned by the mine, bought their food from stores owned by the mine, and often were not paid in dollars but in company scrip, currency minted by mine owners, who then controlled its value. In 1947, Kentucky folksinger Merle Travis immortalized the situation in his song "Sixteen Tons." The song's refrain went:

You load sixteen tons, and what do you get?

Another day older and deeper in debt.

St. Peter, don't you call me, 'cause I can't go....

I owe my soul to the company store.

and their allies, the state's economy began to rely on industry more than agriculture. The nation as a whole was becoming more industrialized, and Kentucky coal was an important resource to fuel the growing economy. By the 1960s, Kentucky was producing almost as much coal as West Virginia, the leading U.S. coal producer at that time.

The period after World War II brought a new emphasis on civil rights. Across the country African Americans were challenging racial inequalities. Kentucky was a segregated state, with separate schools for African-American and white children and laws that made African Americans second-class citizens. African Americans in Kentucky began to demand fair treatment and led the way in bringing about a number of important changes.

In 1948, hospitals in Louisville began to desegregate, and the main branch of the public library in the city was integrated. The first state school to desegregate was the University of Kentucky, which admitted its first African-American graduate student in 1949. The remainder of the state's public colleges were integrated in 1955.

The state passed the Kentucky Civil Rights Act in 1966. It was described by Martin Luther King, Jr., as "the strongest and most comprehensive civil rights bill passed by a Southern state." The law made it illegal to discriminate against anyone on the basis of race in work or public accommodations, such as buses and restaurants.

Sharecroppers' Plight

Many Kentucky farmers worked as sharecroppers, renting the land they farmed from landowners. The landowners required a certain share of the value of the annual crop as payment. During the year sharecroppers would have to borrow money to buy seeds and equipment, as well as food and clothes for their families. They hoped that at harvest time they would be able to sell their crops for enough money to pay off their debts and have a little extra. Many sharecroppers, however, were always in debt to landlords and merchants. They lived in desperate poverty, without basic services.

◄ Kentucky's coal industry boomed during World War II. This picture, taken in July 1944, shows two coal miners near a freight yard filled with trains carrying coal.

In 1967, one of the leaders of Kentucky's Civil Rights movement, Georgia Powers, became the first African American and the first woman elected to the Kentucky State Senate. Powers served for twenty years and introduced legislation to ensure social equality for Kentuckians.

The Federal Coal Mine Health and Safety Act was passed in 1969 to protect miners from the hazardous conditions of their work. Mines were often dangerous places. Cave-ins and explosions killed hundreds of workers over the years. Black lung disease, contracted from breathing coal dust, killed many more. Kentucky's coal mining industry still thrives, although many miners in the eastern part of the state still live in poverty, and black lung disease continues to be a problem.

During the 1970s, Kentucky became the nation's leading producer of coal, a position it held until Wyoming displaced it in the late 1980s. In the 1990s, Kentucky's economy became more diversified and now includes many jobs in the service sector and technology, as well as manufacturing. In 1999, the state launched the Kentucky Virtual University, which has become a model for adult education and distance learning, enabling people who cannot get to a university campus to read books, earn college degrees, and enrich their lives. Even as Kentucky moves into the future, it continues to honor its past with a commitment to the folk cultures and values of its people.

▼ Georgia Powers (*center*) is flanked by baseball great Jackie Robinson (*left*) and Martin Luther King, Jr., (*right*) at a rally she organized in 1964 to fight for equal access to public accommodations.

The World's Garden

> The Englishman points with pride to Stratford-on-Avon, the home of Shakespeare, the world's greatest poet. The American is equally proud of Mt. Vernon, the home of Washington, 'Father of his country'; and we Kentuckians believe our State to be the garden spot of the world.
>
> — *Alexander Walters, bishop of the African Methodist Episcopal Zion Church, in* My Life and Work, *1917*

Kentuckians live mainly in small cities and towns and in rural areas. The state has few large cities. Overall the state is fairly sparsely populated, with an average of 101.7 people per square mile (39 per sq km). Although the national average is only 79.6 people per square mile (30.7 per sq km), Kentucky is much less densely populated than highly developed states such as California. As of 2000, the U.S. Census determined that the state has a total population of 4,041,769, up 9.7 percent from 1990. The median age in Kentucky is 35.9 years, which is about one-half year older than the national median of 35.3 years.

Age Distribution in Kentucky
(2000 Census)

Age	Population
0–4	265,901
5–19	847,743
20–24	283,032
25–44	1,210,773
45–64	929,527
65 & over	504,793

Across One Hundred Years

Kentucky's three largest foreign-born groups for 1890 and 1990

1890
Germany 32,620
Ireland 13,926
England 4,158

Total state population: 1,858,635
Total foreign-born: 59,356 (3%)

1990
Germany 5,118
United Kingdom 2,281
Korea 2,082

Total state population: 3,685,296
Total foreign-born: 34,119 (1%)

Patterns of Immigration

The total number of people who immigrated to Kentucky in 1998 was 2,017. Of that number the largest immigrant groups were from Cuba (12.0%), Vietnam (9.7%), and Mexico (7.0%).

Where Do Kentuckians Live?

Slightly more Kentuckians — 52 percent — live in urban rather than rural areas. The trend toward urbanization began as people were drawn to the north-central part of the state. This area, around the cities of Louisville and Lexington, Kentucky, and including Cincinnati, Ohio, is known as the Golden Triangle because it is the center of much of the state's economic activity. Louisville and Lexington are the only cities in Kentucky with populations greater than one hundred thousand. Meanwhile, urbanization helps account for the recent population losses in the rural eastern and western corners of the state.

▲ Country stores like this one in the town of Rabbit Hash have been a central part of rural Kentucky life since the state's earliest days. More than just a place to buy necessities, the general store was a place to meet friends and find out the latest news. This role was especially essential in the days before electricity and telephones were extended into rural areas.

Ethnic Diversity

Kentucky has been home to a variety of ethnic groups over the course of its history, including Scottish, Irish, English, Welsh, and German immigrants in the eighteenth and nineteenth centuries. Today its population is largely homogeneous. Just over 90 percent of the residents are white and 99.2 percent were born in the United States. African Americans make up a little more than 7 percent of the population. This was not always the case, however. In the 1860s, as much as one-fourth of Kentucky's population was

Heritage and Background, Kentucky   Year 2000

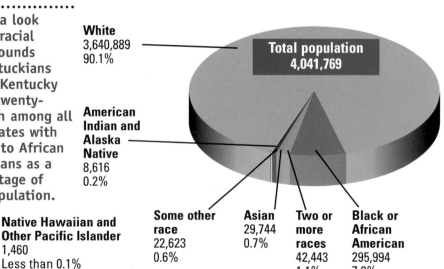

▶ Here's a look at the racial backgrounds of Kentuckians today. Kentucky ranks twenty-seventh among all U.S. states with regard to African Americans as a percentage of the population.

White 3,640,889 90.1%

Total population 4,041,769

American Indian and Alaska Native 8,616 0.2%

Native Hawaiian and Other Pacific Islander 1,460 Less than 0.1%

Some other race 22,623 0.6%

Asian 29,744 0.7%

Two or more races 42,443 1.1%

Black or African American 295,994 7.3%

Note: 1.5% (59,939) of the population identify themselves as **Hispanic** or **Latino,** a cultural designation that crosses racial lines. Hispanics and Latinos are counted in this category as well as the racial category of their choice.

◀ The Louisville sky-
line as seen from
across the Ohio
River. Louisville
is Kentucky's
second-largest city.

African-American. Most African Americans were slaves. A
small number of free African Americans lived in the state,
mostly in urban areas, where they worked as craftspeople and
did much to support the spread of abolitionist ideas. When
the Emancipation Proclamation ended slavery in 1863, many
African Americans left for northern states, where they hoped
to find less prejudice and more economic opportunity.

Religion

Approximately 90 percent of Kentuckians identify themselves
as Christians. Among this group the largest denomination
is Baptist, accounting for 43 percent of the state's total
population. Nearly 7 percent of the state's residents are
Methodists, 2 percent are Pentecostals, and approximately
1 percent are Presbyterians. Close to 13 percent of
Kentuckians are Roman Catholic. Among the 10 percent of
the population who do not identify themselves as Christian
are the 3 percent who are agnostic, neither believing nor
disbelieving in God; the 3 percent who are Jewish; and the
0.1 percent who are practicing Buddhists. There are six
Islamic centers in the state, mostly in Louisville.

Education

Kentucky's
educational system
had difficult
beginnings. Although
there was some public
education in the state
before the Civil War,
public schools
essentially ceased
to exist during

Educational Levels of Kentucky Workers (age 25 and over)	
Less than 9th grade	442,579
9th to 12th grade, no diploma	383,278
High school graduate, including equivalency	741,012
Some college, no degree or associate degree	448,873
Bachelor's degree	189,539
Graduate or professional degree	128,588

Reconstruction. At the start of the twentieth century, illiteracy was a major problem in Kentucky. The need for reform became even greater as the state's economy moved away from agriculture toward greater industrialization because literate workers were required to fill new jobs. In 1908, the Sullivan Law was passed, overhauling the public school system. The law established new school districts across the state and made it a requirement that all children attend school between the ages of seven and fourteen. Perhaps most importantly the law also established a property tax to pay for the state's school system, the first time education had been funded by law in Kentucky.

While the Sullivan Law was an important first step, serious inequities among school districts remained. Districts were funded by property taxes collected within each county, which meant that the richer districts had more resources than the poorer ones. The quality of education in the different school districts reflected this inequality and, over time, the performance of the poorer districts worsened.

In the 1980s, sixty-six school districts joined together to sue the state to change the way that schools were funded. The case went all the way to the Kentucky Supreme Court, which ruled in 1989 that the educational system in Kentucky was unconstitutional. In response the General Assembly began a review of the public schools and, in 1990, it passed the Kentucky Education Reform Act (KERA), one of the most sweeping education reform bills in U.S. history. It completely restructured the way school funds are distributed, making sure each district receives a comparable amount of funding, despite regional variations in property tax amounts. Today, children between the ages of six and sixteen must remain in school. Sixteen-year-olds may only leave school with the permission of a parent.

◄ In 1956, Kentucky classrooms were desegregated for the first time. Here, schoolchildren are shown entering a Louisville elementary school.

Bluegrass Prairies

Heaven is a Kentucky of a place.
— *An anonymous preacher quoted in*
The WPA Guide to Kentucky, *1939*

Kentucky is divided into five geographic regions. Going from west to east, the first of these areas is the Jackson Purchase, so called because it was added to the state in 1818 when Andrew Jackson bought the land from the Chickasaw. East of this lies the Western Coal Field, a hilly region of rich farmland. The Pennyroyal Region surrounds the Western Coal Field on the western, southern, and eastern sides, snaking off to the northeast. Named for a type of mint that grows throughout the area, the Pennyroyal is known for limestone deposits and sandstone cliffs. Just above and to the east of the Pennyroyal is the Bluegrass Region, filled with lush farmland, the site of many of Kentucky's famous horse farms. Finally, in the eastern portion of the state, is the Eastern Coal Field, a mountainous area that includes the state's highest point, Black Mountain. At its widest points the state measures 426 miles (685 km) across and 174 miles (280 km) north to south.

Lakes and Rivers

With the exception of its southern border, Kentucky is bordered by rivers. To the west lies the mighty Mississippi; the Ohio is to the north; and the Big Sandy and the Tug

Highest Point
Black Mountain
4,145 feet (1,264 m) above sea level

▼ *From left to right:* the Roebling Suspension Bridge in Covington; 200-year-old limestone fences in the Bluegrass Region; thorough-breds graze on a horse farm near Lexington; Daniel Boone National Forest; the Palisades, limestone cliffs along the Kentucky River; the gray squirrel, the state wild animal.

Fork are in the east. Within the state, the Kentucky River flows westward from the mountains of eastern Kentucky to the Ohio River. Until the railroads were constructed in the mid- to late-1800s, rivers and streams were the primary means of transporting goods to markets. The Ohio and Mississippi Rivers were particularly important, as they connected Kentucky to cities in Ohio and Indiana and to ports in the South.

There are few natural lakes in Kentucky, but there are more than fifty artificially created lakes and reservoirs. Lake Cumberland was created in 1952 on the Cumberland River. Just over 50,000 acres (20,235 ha) in area, the lake contains General Burnside State Park, the only park in Kentucky that exists entirely upon an island. Today, the largest lake in the state is Kentucky Lake, which was created when the Kentucky Dam was built in the 1940s. It covers almost 160,000 acres (65,000 ha) and was the largest human-made created lake in the world when it was created in 1944.

Plains and Flatlands

The Bluegrass Region and the Western Coal Field are generally hilly, but the Jackson Purchase is characterized by floodplains that surround the tributaries of the Mississippi River. The flatlands near the Mississippi are fertile farmland thanks to silt deposited by the river's waters. The river's waters are not always so benevolent — the region is subject to severe flooding whenever the Mississippi overflows.

Plant Life

Plants that thrive in Kentucky include Kentucky glade grass, Cumberland rosinweed, and two varieties of goldenrod, the state flower. Kentucky is known for the bluegrass that grows throughout the central part of the

Largest Lakes
Kentucky Lake
158,080 acres
(63,975 ha)

Lake Barkley
57,920 acres
(23,440 ha)

Lake Cumberland
50,250 acres
(20,336 ha)

Major Rivers
Ohio River
981 miles (1,578 km)

Cumberland River
720 miles (1,158 km)

Kentucky River
259 miles (417 km)

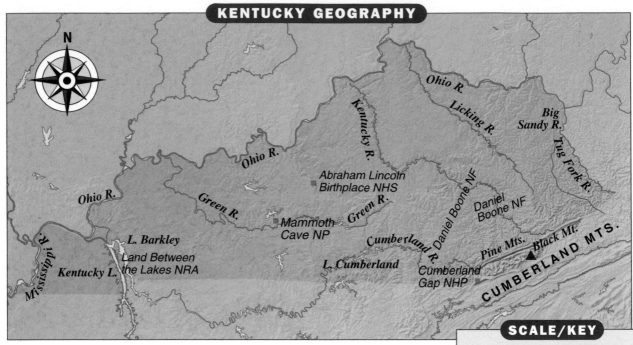

state. Bluegrass is not native to the continent, however, and was probably carried over to the United States by the first settlers from Europe, where it is also plentiful. The grass grows to between 18 and 24 inches (46 to 61 centimeters) and ranges in color from green to deep bluish green.

Before European settlement, most of Kentucky was covered by forests. Today, forests cover nearly half of the state's land area. During the nineteenth and twentieth centuries, many native forests were cut down for use in the lumber industry. Major reforesting projects since then have helped to replace trees. Among the trees that grow in Kentucky are beech, basswood, oak, sugar maple, eastern hemlock, sycamore, shagbark hickory, and pine. The tallest species of tree in Kentucky is the tulip tree, a flowering tree that can grow to 190 feet (58 m) high. The Kentucky coffee tree produces brown beans that were used to make coffee during the colonial era.

Kentucky's wild flowering plants include violets, anemones, and asters. Dogwoods, azaleas, rhododendrons, magnolias, and sassafrases are among the flowering shrubs that brighten up Kentucky's wilderness areas.

Animals

The wild animal population of Kentucky includes animals as large as black bears and as small as voles. The red wolf was once a common sight in the state and has recently been

SCALE/KEY

| 0 | 100 Miles |
| 0 | 100 Kilometers |

NF	National Forest
NHP	National Historic Park
NHS	National Historic Site
NP	National Park
NRA	National Recreation Area
▲	Highest Point
	Mountains

reintroduced. The wolf shares terrain with minks and gray and red foxes. Among the state's rodents are chipmunks, muskrats, and squirrels. Squirrels have historically been hunted as game in Kentucky.

Among the many species of birds that can be found in Kentucky are game birds, such as the wild turkey and the ring-necked pheasant. Great blue herons, yellow-bellied sapsuckers, and brown thrashers also make Kentucky home.

There are more than two hundred fish species in the state's extensive network of lakes, rivers, and streams, including catfish, bluegill, crappie, and two kinds of largemouth bass.

Climate

Situated between the coastal states and the nation's heartland, Kentucky is buffered from extreme weather conditions. There are occasional droughts and floods in the state, and tornadoes occur each year. In 1974, an outbreak of tornadoes struck the state twenty-six times in nine hours, causing approximately $110 million in damages. The state runs a disaster center web site to keep residents informed of dangerous weather conditions.

Average January temperature
Jackson: 32.8°F (0°C)
Paducah: 32.6°F (0°C)

Average July temperature
Jackson: 74.6°F (24°C)
Paducah: 78.8°F (26°C)

Average yearly rainfall
Jackson: 50 inches (129 cm)
Paducah: 49 inches (126 cm)

Average yearly snowfall
Jackson: 24.2 inches (62 cm)
Paducah: 10.9 inches (28 cm)

▼ Kentucky Lake, created by the formation of the Kentucky Dam, is home to abundant wildlife.

A Land That Provides

> For more than two centuries Kentuckians have based their domestic economy and culture upon the land and its natural resources.
> — The Kentucky Encyclopedia, *1992*

At the end of the Civil War, most Kentuckians worked on farms. By the outbreak of World War II, only about a third of them did. By 1990, however, less than 5 percent of the state's population was employed in agriculture. By the end of the twentieth century, manufacturing's position as the major sector in the state's economy had been confirmed.

Manufacturing

Factory owners have long been motivated to locate their factories in Kentucky because of the coal that the state produces, which can be used to power factory machinery. Kentucky also offers another source of energy; dams that have been built on its rivers provide hydroelectric power. In 1986, the Japanese auto manufacturer Toyota opened a plant in Georgetown, in the eastern part of the state. Soon more than seventy auto-parts companies opened nearby, creating jobs for local workers. Today, Kentucky is the third-largest automobile producer and is home to major Toyota, GM, and Ford plants. Nearly 10 percent of all cars and trucks manufactured in the United States come from Kentucky factories. Other major industries in the state produce machinery, electronics, metals, food products, and chemicals.

Nearly one-quarter of the income earned from food processing in Kentucky is earned through the production of beverages. The most important is whiskey, particularly bourbon, an alcoholic beverage for which the state is famous. Kentucky produces more whiskey than any other state.

Top Employers
(of workers age sixteen and over)

Employer	Percent
Services	29.5%
Wholesale and retail trade	21.5%
Manufacturing	18.9%
Transportation, communications, and other public utilities	8.6%
Construction	6.9%
Finance, insurance, and real estate	6.5%
Public Administration	5.4%
Agriculture, forestry, and fisheries	2.4%
Mining	0.3%

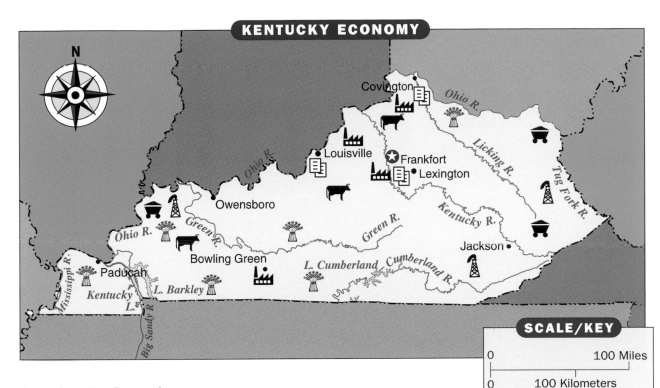

KENTUCKY ECONOMY

Service Industries

As is true across the nation, the service industries have become increasingly important to Kentucky's economy. Today, they are the second-largest economic sector in the state. Unlike other parts of the country, however, Kentucky has relatively few jobs in high-paying service sectors such as finance and insurance. Instead, Kentucky's service jobs tend to be in areas such as transportation and retail sales. As a result, earnings in Kentucky tend to be on the low side of the national average.

SCALE/KEY

0 — 100 Miles
0 — 100 Kilometers

- 🐂 Cattle
- Farming
- 🏭 Manufacturing
- Mining
- Oil/Natural Gas
- Services
- Urban Areas

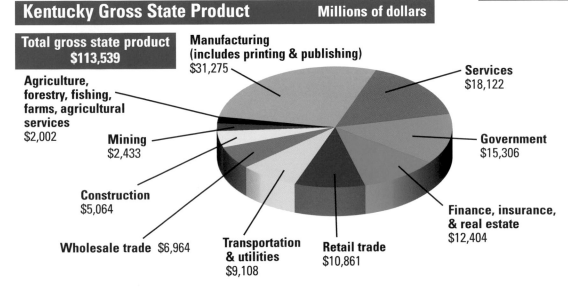

Kentucky Gross State Product   Millions of dollars

Total gross state product $113,539

Manufacturing (includes printing & publishing) $31,275

Services $18,122

Government $15,306

Finance, insurance, & real estate $12,404

Retail trade $10,861

Transportation & utilities $9,108

Wholesale trade $6,964

Construction $5,064

Mining $2,433

Agriculture, forestry, fishing, farms, agricultural services $2,002

Ever since Toyota opened a plant in Georgetown in 1986, Kentucky has been a powerhouse in the automobile industry. As more manufacturers opened plants and auto-parts companies in the state, Kentucky rose to become the nation's third-largest car producer. Here, an employee at Toyota's Georgetown plant inspects a vehicle.

Agriculture

Although only a small percentage of the state's population is involved in agriculture, Kentucky still has ninety thousand farms, the fourth-greatest number of farms in any state in the nation. The majority of these farms — 57 percent — do not earn more than $10,000 per year. The most profitable crop is tobacco; Kentucky ranks second after North Carolina in tobacco production. Kentucky tobacco farmers primarily produce burley and dark leaf tobacco. Kentucky farmers also grow corn and soybeans, mostly in the western part of the state.

Beef cattle are the state's most valuable source of livestock income. Dairy cows, poultry, and hogs are also raised for profit. The most famous livestock in Kentucky, however, are thoroughbred horses. Thoroughbreds are raised in the Bluegrass Region and can cost several hundred thousand dollars each.

Corn is grown in western Kentucky, both for human consumption and for livestock feed.

Mining

Since the mid-1800s, coal mines have been very important to Kentucky's economy. Coal brought a much-needed boost to the state's economy in the late nineteenth century and continues in importance today. In the 1990s, annual income from mining exceeded $4 billion. Much of the mining has been strip mining, wherein surface soil is stripped away to

reveal the coal beneath. Strip-mining causes erosion of soil and also pollutes water sources. In 1977, federal law required mining companies to restore land to its original condition — or as close as possible — after an area has been strip-mined. In places such as Hopkins and Pike Counties, hillsides are now being restored to their original beauty as mining companies cover stripped areas with grass and landscaping.

Although coal is by far the most important product of mining in the state, it is not the only valuable substance collected there. Petroleum and natural gas are also extracted from under the coal fields in the eastern and western parts of the state. Crushed stone is another important product of Kentucky's mining industry.

▲ Kentucky has a multi-billion dollar beef cattle industry, making cattle the number one earner among state livestock. With 1.1 million animals, Kentucky is also the nation's largest producer of beef cattle east of the Mississippi.

Tourism

Since the 1950s, tourists have been spending a lot of time and money in Kentucky. Forty-nine state parks and five nationally designated outdoor recreation areas, as well as hundreds of historical and cultural attractions, draw visitors to the state. Tourism brings nearly $9 billion into the state each year. Tourism services are the state's second-largest employer and third-largest revenue-producing industry.

Made in Kentucky

Leading farm products and crops
Tobacco
Thoroughbred horses
Corn
Soybeans
Beef cattle

Other products
Coal
Machinery
Motor vehicles
Electronic equipment
Chemicals
Processed food and beverages

Major Airports		
Airport	**Location**	**Passengers per year (2000)**
Cincinnati/Northern Kentucky International	Hebron (Cincinnati, Ohio)	22,537,525
Louisville International	Louisville	3,954,243
Blue Grass Airport	Lexington	1,006,646

A Political People

> Kentucky cannot claim first place in political importance, but it tops the list in its keen enjoyment of politics for its own sake. It takes the average Kentuckian only a matter of moments to dispose of the weather and personal health, but he never tires of a political discussion.
>
> — The WPA Guide to Kentucky, *1939*

K entucky has had four constitutions, which were adopted in 1792, 1799, 1850, and 1891. The first provided a basic outline of the state government's structure and a bill of rights. The 1799 constitution revised the first, giving more power to individuals by establishing direct elections but taking away freed slaves' right to vote. The 1850 constitution sought to limit the spending powers of the legislature, which had run up a large debt. The 1891 constitution again sought to limit the power of state government and, as a result, the legislative branch was further weakened. The constitution divides the power of state government among the executive, legislative, and judicial branches.

The Executive Branch

The executive branch of the Kentucky state government includes seven elected officials. The governor and lieutenant governor, elected together, serve at the head of government. The other elected offices are the attorney general, auditor of public accounts, state treasurer, secretary of state, and commissioner of agriculture.

The governor appoints people to cabinet posts and to jobs in many agencies and departments, such as the Department of Education and the Department of Agriculture. The relationship between the executive and legislative branches in Kentucky is a little different from that in other states. Kentucky's governor has more power

State Constitution

When he shall convene the General Assembly it shall be by proclamation, stating the subjects to be considered, and no other shall be considered.

— *from Section 80 of the 1891 Kentucky State Constitution, describing the governor's power to call special sessions of the assembly*

than most other state governors, partly because of unusual rules that effectively limit how much the state's legislative branch can do. For example, Kentucky governors can make many appointments without legislative approval, while in many states, appointments to important positions must be reviewed by the state legislature. The governor of Kentucky also makes an unusually high number of appointments.

The Legislative Branch

The Kentucky General Assembly has two houses, a senate and a house of representatives. The assembly meets for a thirty-day session in odd-numbered years and a sixty-day session in even-numbered years. Special sessions must be called by the governor. For most of Kentucky's history, the assembly met only in even-numbered years. This restriction severely limited the assembly's scope and power. Kentucky voters, however, repeatedly rejected constitutional amendments that would allow the assembly to meet every year.

Since the mid-1900s, the assembly has worked to get around these restrictions. In 1948, the assembly created the Legislative Research Commission (LRC), which is designed to allow work to be done between sessions. The LRC is a sixteen-member panel that includes the Democratic and Republican leaders from the senate and the house of representatives. It produces reports, drafts bills, and

▲ Kentucky's capitol is its fourth since statehood. The building was finished in 1910 and cost $1.8 million.

Elected Posts in the Executive Branch		
Office	**Length of Term**	**Term Limits**
Governor	4 years	2 terms
Lieutenant Governor	4 years	2 terms
Auditor	4 years	2 terms
Treasurer	4 years	2 terms
Attorney General	4 years	2 terms
Secretary of State	4 years	2 terms
Commissioner of Agriculture	4 years	2 terms

performs other functions in support of the legislature. Until 1979, it also held conferences to orient new assembly members and to allow for leadership elections. In 1979, the constitution was amended to allow the assembly to hold organizational meetings in odd-numbered years.

In 1968, the assembly created a system under which committees may perform some work between sessions. New committees were created in the 1970s to review the work of the executive branch. In the 1970s, the legislature also ended the practice of rubber-stamping, or approving without debate, the governor's budget.

The Judicial Branch

The state's first constitution did not provide any details regarding a court system. Instead, the legislature created a three-member court of appeals, the highest court in the state. The three judges were appointed to life terms by the governor. The 1850 constitution expanded the court to four members and caused them to be elected rather than appointed. Additional changes, made in 1975, created a supreme court as the highest court in the state. Seven justices are elected from supreme court districts for eight-year terms. One justice is chosen by the supreme court members to serve a four-year term as chief justice. Below the supreme court is the court of appeals, which has thirteen associate justices and a chief justice, all of whom are elected to eight-year terms. The lowest court in the state is the circuit court, to which judges are elected for eight-year terms. Circuit courts handle both criminal cases and civil cases that involve claims of more than $4,000. There are ninety-seven district circuit judges in Kentucky's fifty-six judicial districts.

Common Good

Kentucky is officially a commonwealth rather than a state. The word *commonwealth* dates to the time of Oliver Cromwell, a seventeenth-century English statesman, and comes from the word *commonweal*, meaning "the public good." Kentucky is the only commonwealth among the fifty states that was not one of the original thirteen colonies. The other three are Massachusetts, Pennsylvania, and Virginia.

▼ Kentucky's third capitol, used between 1830 and 1910, today houses the Kentucky Historical Society.

The White House via Kentucky

ABRAHAM LINCOLN (1861–1865)

Abraham Lincoln, the sixteenth president of the United States, spent his early years in rural Kentucky. His family moved to Indiana when he was seven, ultimately settling in Illinois, where Lincoln remained for most of his life. Lincoln only attended school for a year, but he loved to read and learned to be an eloquent speaker.

Lincoln won a seat in the state legislature in 1834 and began practicing law in Springfield, Illinois, in 1837. He served one term in the U.S. House of Representatives and became known for his opposition to slavery. In the 1850s, he joined the new Republican party and ran for the U.S. Senate in 1858 against Democrat Stephen A. Douglas. Their debates over slavery gained national attention. Lincoln lost the election but established himself in the Republican party and became its nominee for president two years later. Running against Douglas again, Lincoln gave eloquent speeches that helped him win the election.

Lincoln became president, and the Civil War began. Some Southern states seceded before he even took office. His entire presidency would be focused on winning the war and saving the Union. Although he is not considered a great military strategist, Lincoln was a cunning politician, and this served him well during the most difficult period in the nation's history. His leadership was critical throughout the war. Five days after the Confederacy's surrender, he was assassinated by John Wilkes Booth while attending a performance at Ford's Theater in Washington, D.C.

Local Government

Most of Kentucky's 120 counties are governed by fiscal courts. Fiscal courts are composed of elected representatives who transact the business of the county. Fiscal courts may be composed of a county judge and commissioners elected at large, or a county judge and justices of the peace elected from districts. The county judge is the chief executive of the county.

Municipal areas are governed in one of three ways. Some municipalities have a mayor and city council, while others have a commission and city manager or a council and city manager.

General Assembly			
House	Number of Members	Length of Term	Term Limits
Senate	38 senators	4 years	none
House of Representatives	100 representatives	2 years	none

Thoroughbred Country

> If Jack Nicklaus can win the
> Masters at forty-six, I can win the
> Kentucky Derby at fifty-four.
> — *Willie Shoemaker, jockey*

Kentucky's hills and valleys contain a variety of breathtaking scenery ready to be enjoyed by outdoor enthusiasts. In particular, the white water of Kentucky's wild rivers is a beacon for expert canoeists. Bikers can explore the Great River Road, a bike trail that runs from Canada to the Gulf of Mexico as it follows the course of the Mississippi River.

State and National Parks

Kentucky maintains a wide variety of parks. They range from the 15-acre (6-ha) Old Fort Harrod State Park to the 4,600-acre (1,862-ha) Breaks Interstate Park, a joint venture with Virginia that lies on the border between the two states. At Cumberland Falls State Resort Park, mist from the waterfall when the moon is full creates a "moonbow" — a rainbow created by moonlight — that is an exceedingly rare phenomenon. John James Audubon State Park includes a museum housing original prints from the artist's *Birds of America*. General Burnside State Park is a 430-acre (174-ha) island in Lake Cumberland.

Mammoth Cave National Park, near Bowling Green, hosts 1.8 million visitors a year. Above ground the park is an 80-square-mile (207-sq-km) region of hills and valleys. It features more than 60 miles (97 km) of hiking trails, as well as canoeing and fishing on the Green River. The most popular feature of the park is the cave itself. The longest known cave system in the world, it has more than 340 miles (547 km) of caverns and passageways. Troglobites such as eyeless shrimp and cave beetles spend their whole lives in the dark cave.

DID YOU KNOW?

Kaelin's in Louisville claims to be the first restaurant to have served a cheese-topped hamburger. A menu dating back to 1934 proves that the restaurant is at least in the running for this history-making event. An application to trademark the word "cheeseburger" was filed in Denver, Colorado, in 1935 by the owner of the Humpty-Dumpty Barrel Drive-In.

The Civil War

Kentuckians remember their Civil War heritage at the many battle sites around the state, including fifty-one that are part of the national Civil War Discovery Trail. The trail leads visitors to more than five hundred sites in twenty-eight states. Among Kentucky's Civil War sites is the Perryville Battlefield State Historic Site. Each year, Civil War enthusiasts reenact the 1862 Battle of Perryville, in which nearly forty thousand Union and Confederate troops engaged.

Museums

Among the many museums in Kentucky is the Behringer-Crawford Museum in Covington, which houses exhibits on the natural and cultural history of northern Kentucky. The Kentucky Folk Art Center, at Morehead State University in Morehead, celebrates the work of local folk artists and

▼ A spelunker examines stalactite formations in Kentucky's Mammoth Cave.

craftspeople. In Frankfort, the Kentucky Historical Society maintains both the Kentucky History Center, and the Kentucky Military History Museum, giving visitors a glimpse into the history of the state during both war and peacetime. There are many historic houses in the state that can be toured, including a house in Lexington where Mary Todd Lincoln, the wife of U.S. president Abraham Lincoln, lived when she was a child.

The Louisville Science Center offers exhibits on space, the human body, and the environment, as well as a rock-climbing wall. In Benham, the Kentucky Coal Mining Museum exhibits artifacts related to the coal industry, including train cars used to carry miners underground, mining tools, and a two-ton block of coal.

Music

Kentucky has a rich musical heritage dating back to its earliest days. The first music school in the state was established in 1795. The Louisville Orchestra was founded in 1937 and became known in the 1950s for commissioning and recording new works by contemporary composers. Many of the pieces the orchestra commissioned have become standards. The Louisville Orchestra made the first recordings of works by composers Aaron Copland, Elliott Carter, and others. The Kentucky Opera was founded in 1952, and the Lexington Philharmonic in 1965. Kentucky, however, is certainly better known for its contributions to country music, especially for the development of the musical style known as bluegrass.

Bluegrass developed out of acoustic country music in the mid-twentieth century and usually features a five-person band consisting of fiddle (violin), bass fiddle (acoustic bass), banjo, mandolin, and guitar. Songs often feature solo or harmonized vocals and extremely fast, intricate instrumental solos.

The style is named after a band from the 1940s called Bill Monroe and the Blue Grass Boys. Monroe, a Kentucky native, is known as the "Father of Bluegrass Music." The term *bluegrass* did not come into wide use until the 1960s.

▲ Bluegrass legend Bill Monroe plays a mandolin in a field in Rosine, Kentucky. Sometimes called the "Father of Bluegrass Music," Monroe absorbed the elements of traditional country and gospel music as a child, learning to play the mandolin. He began performing on the radio with his brother Charlie in the 1920s, and in the 1930s formed his own band, the Blue Grass Boys. Monroe was inducted into the Country Music Hall of Fame in 1970 and died in 1996.

At that time electrically amplified instruments were used by many country musicians, because of the influence of rock and roll. Music purists wanted to find a way to distinguish the music exemplified by Monroe from the popular new style.

Literary Traditions

An impressive number of poets, novelists, and short-story writers have found literary inspiration in their home state of Kentucky. Robert Penn Warren, poet and novelist from Guthrie, won three Pulitzer Prizes and was the first U.S. Poet Laureate. He is probably best known for his novel about Louisiana politics, *All the King's Men* (1946), but many of his works, including the novel *World Enough and Time* (1950), are set in Kentucky. Jesse Stuart drew on his experiences growing up in and later returning to the mountains of eastern Kentucky to write poetry, novels, and short stories that are beloved by readers of all ages. Other writers especially identified with Kentucky include Elizabeth Hardwick and Bobbie Ann Mason.

Performing Arts

Theater is flourishing in Kentucky. The Actors Theatre of Louisville is home to the annual Humana Festival of New American Plays. Many plays performed for the first time at this festival go on to be produced in New York and other large cities.

The Lexington Children's Theatre, also known as the State Children's Theatre of Kentucky, is one of the oldest theaters for children in the nation. The Kentucky Shakespeare Festival, founded in 1960, offers free performances of plays by Shakespeare in Louisville's Central Park. Kentucky legends and historical events are the inspiration for many outdoor dramas performed throughout the state. The life of Daniel Boone on the Kentucky frontier is the subject of a play presented in Harrodsburg every summer. The songs of Stephen Foster, the nineteenth-century songwriter, are featured in *Stephen Foster — The Musical,* performed annually in Bardstown.

▲ The Shaker village of Pleasant Hill is located near Harrodsburg. The Shakers are members of a sect of Christians that was founded in Kentucky in the early nineteenth century. The Shakers are known for their simplicity and devotion, both of which are reflected in their beautiful furniture and crafts.

Kentucky Shakers

In the first decade of the 1800s, Shakers founded two settlements in Kentucky — Pleasant Hill and South Union. Both communities lasted for more than one hundred years. The Shakers, named for the way they trembled during their intense prayer and devotional dancing, were Christians who believed in sharing property and in renouncing many of the world's pleasures. Members became famous for the simple beauty and ingenuity of the many items they made and invented. Their furniture, in particular, was both beautiful and practical and embodied the Shaker belief that the act of making an object, and making it well, was a form of prayer.

Today, the Shaker Village of Pleasant Hill is a National Historic Landmark. Once home to as many as five hundred people, the last remaining Pleasant Hill Shaker died in 1923. Visitors can take part in a riverboat tour as well as explore the extensive grounds and buildings. The Shaker Museum in South Union highlights the many products the Shakers made and sold, including flower and vegetable seeds, brooms, baskets, linen, and silk.

Sports

Perhaps the most famous institution in all Kentucky is the "Run for the Roses," the Kentucky Derby. Held the first Saturday in May, the Derby is easily the best-known horse race in the United States. Only three-year-old horses are eligible to compete in the Kentucky Derby. It has been run

▲ Shakers are famous for the simple elegance of their crafts. Their oval boxes (which they first made in about 1800) are perfect examples of Shaker work. Woods like birch and cherry were commonly used, with the sides held together by metal tacks.

DID YOU KNOW?

Man o' War, perhaps the greatest thoroughbred in racing history, never ran in the Kentucky Derby. He won every race he ran, including the Preakness and Belmont Stakes, except for one — the Sanford Memorial in 1919. His single loss was to a horse named Upset.

◄ Thoroughbreds thunder toward the homestretch in the 1996 Kentucky Derby.

every year since 1875 and regularly brings more than one hundred thousand spectators to the Churchill Downs racecourse in Louisville. The Derby is part of a two-week festival that includes a balloon race and the Great Steamboat Race. Horses that compete in the Derby usually go on to run in two other races, the Preakness and the Belmont Stakes. To win all three is to win the Triple Crown, the pinnacle of U.S. horse racing.

The fastest Derby horse ever was Secretariat. In 1973, he completed the 1.25-mile (2-km) track in just 1 minute 59.4 seconds — an average speed of 37.68 miles (60.6 km) per hour. He also went on to win the Triple Crown.

Not surprisingly, Kentucky is home to many of the nation's top horse breeders. The Bluegrass Region has an abundance of minerals in its soil and water that contribute to the growth of strong but light bones and tendons in foals, or young horses. As a result, horses raised in the region tend to have an advantage over horses raised in other places. The advantage is so great that some races simply disqualify horses bred in Kentucky.

In 1978, the Kentucky Horse Park was opened near Lexington. Attractions include a visitors' center, the International Museum of the Horse, a model farm, a number of exhibits and shows, and a resort campground. The park is a major tourist attraction for the area.

In a state with no major professional sports teams, athletic programs from the two largest universities generate much local support. Both the University of Kentucky and the University of Louisville have men's basketball programs with winning traditions. Coach Rick Pitino, who led the Kentucky Wildcats during their NCAA championship run in 1996, signed with Louisville in 2001.

Rupp Arena

In an age when many large sports venues are named for corporate sponsors, the Rupp Arena, home to the famed University of Kentucky Wildcat basketball team, is an exception. This sports facility, built in 1975, stands as a monument to Adolph Rupp. Beginning in 1930, Coach Rupp led his Wildcats to an astounding 875 victories over his 41-year career. Called "The Baron of Bluegrass," Rupp forged his champions from local materials, finding more than 80 percent of his talented players in the nearby Kentucky hills.

Leaders and Legends

> I didn't have any choice as to where
> I was born, but if I had had my choice,
> I would have chosen Kentucky.
>
> —from "Kentucky Is My Land" (1952) by Jesse Stuart,
> Kentucky Poet Laureate, 1954–1984

Following are only a few of the thousands of people who were born, died, or spent much of their lives in Kentucky and made extraordinary contributions to the state and the nation.

DANIEL BOONE

FRONTIERSMAN

BORN: *November 2, 1734, Berks County, PA*
DIED: *September 26, 1820, St. Charles, MO*

Although Daniel Boone might seem like a myth, he was a real person, and he played an important role in the early history of Kentucky. Famous as a hunter, tracker, explorer, and leader of his fellow settlers, he is perhaps the best-known frontiersman in American history. Boone grew up in Berks County, Pennsylvania. When he was 17, his family moved to the Yadkin Valley in North Carolina, where he met his future wife, Rebecca Bryan. In 1755, he joined the British army to participate in the French and Indian War. The following year he and Rebecca married and settled in the Yadkin Valley, but since Boone was an adventurer, he periodically left home to join battles against Native Americans and to explore the frontier. In 1767, he ventured into Kentucky for the first time and quickly became an expert on its terrain. After exploring the region for several years, he moved his family to that wild land west of the Appalachians. In the 1770s, Boone worked for the Transylvania Company, exploring areas and clearing wilderness. Largely due to his leadership, Kentucky was settled. Although he moved from place to place throughout his life, it was Kentucky that he preferred to call home.

JOHN JAMES AUDUBON
ILLUSTRATOR

BORN: *April 26, 1785, Santo Domingo (now Haiti)*
DIED: *January 27, 1851, New York, NY*

Considered the greatest illustrator of North American birds, John James Audubon compiled much of his *Birds of America* while living in Kentucky. He moved to Louisville in 1807 to become a storekeeper. Over the next three years, he made more than two hundred drawings of birds. Fifteen years later he was seriously in debt, and in the financial panic of 1819, he lost his store and took his family to Ohio. Much of the four-volume *Birds of America* had been completed by that time, but publication would not begin until 1827. Famous for their beauty and accurate details, Audubon's drawings have become the standard by which others are judged. Many of his original works are currently held by the museum in John James Audubon State Park in Henderson County.

JEFFERSON DAVIS
CONFEDERATE LEADER

BORN: *June 3, 1808, Davisburg (now Fairview)*
DIED: *December 6, 1889, New Orleans, LA*

The youngest of ten children, Jefferson Davis was born in a log house in rural Kentucky. He moved with his family to Mississippi as a young child but returned to Kentucky to attend Transylvania University in 1823. His political career included terms representing Mississippi in the U.S. House and Senate and an appointment as secretary of war. He resigned from the Senate when Mississippi seceded from the Union in 1861. Less than a month later, he was appointed the first (and only) president of the Confederate States of America by the provisional Confederate Congress. When the Confederacy was defeated in 1865, Davis was captured. Later he traveled to Canada and elsewhere, settling in Tennessee in 1869. In 1881, he completed a book, *The Rise and Fall of the Confederate Government.*

CARRY NATION
TEMPERANCE CAMPAIGNER

BORN: *November 25, 1846, Garrard County*
DIED: *June 9, 1911, Leavenworth, KS*

Carry Moore made her name as a crusader against alcohol. She married an alcoholic, Charles Gloyd, in 1867 but left him almost immediately. Her marriage probably inspired the anti-alcohol campaign that made her famous. When she remarried minister David Nation, she began her campaign. In 1900, she destroyed a saloon in Kansas and soon became known for "hatchetation," destroying saloons with a hatchet. Nation also lectured in favor of women's rights and sex education, and against the use of tobacco.

LOUIS D. BRANDEIS
JURIST

BORN: *November 13, 1856, Louisville*
DIED: *October 5, 1941, Washington, D.C.*

Born and raised in Louisville, Louis D. Brandeis enrolled in Harvard Law School in 1875 and graduated in 1877 with high honors. He practiced law in St. Louis and Boston, and in 1890 he cowrote an article for the *Harvard Law Review* that helped define the legal concept of privacy. He was appointed to the U.S. Supreme Court in 1916, becoming the first Jewish person to serve on the high court. Brandeis was known for decisions that supported civil liberties. He retired from the court in 1939.

D.W. GRIFFITH
FILM DIRECTOR

BORN: *January 22, 1875, Floydsfork (now Crestwood)*
DIED: *July 23, 1948, Hollywood, CA*

One of the most important filmmakers of the Silent Era, David Wark Griffith spent his early years on a farm near Louisville. He started acting in 1896 and appeared in his first film in 1908. He quickly began directing short works and developed a number of innovations, such as close-up and lighting techniques. He made twenty-eight feature films. The most famous was *The Birth of a Nation* (1915), a Civil War epic in which the Ku Klux Klan is portrayed heroically. The movie's controversial nature added to its box office success. *Birth of a Nation* was the first film to be shown in the White House. Woodrow Wilson was president at the time. With the advent of sound films, Griffith stopped making movies.

CASEY JONES
RAILROAD ENGINEER

BORN: *March 14, 1864, Jordan, MO*
DIED: *April 30, 1900, Vaughan, MS*

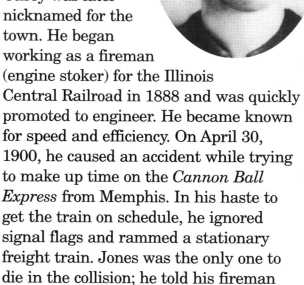

The legendary railroad engineer moved with his family to Cayce (pronounced "casey"), Kentucky, where he spent his youth. Born John Luther Jones, Casey was later nicknamed for the town. He began working as a fireman (engine stoker) for the Illinois Central Railroad in 1888 and was quickly promoted to engineer. He became known for speed and efficiency. On April 30, 1900, he caused an accident while trying to make up time on the *Cannon Ball Express* from Memphis. In his haste to get the train on schedule, he ignored signal flags and rammed a stationary freight train. Jones was the only one to die in the collision; he told his fireman to jump for his life before the crash. A famous folk song commemorates his skill and bravery.

COLONEL SANDERS
RESTAURATEUR

BORN: *September 9, 1890, Henryville, IN*
DIED: *December 16, 1980, Shelbyville*

A pioneer of the fast-food industry, Harland David Sanders quit school after the sixth grade and spent nearly half his life working at odd jobs. In 1929, he opened a gas station and café in Corbin. The tiny lunchroom quickly caught on, and customers flocked in to try Sanders's special fried chicken. The restaurant continued to grow until Interstate 75, built in the 1940s, bypassed the town. Business dropped off, and Sanders had to close the restaurant, but that wasn't the end of the chicken business. He decided to sell franchises, which means allowing people to buy the rights to sell certain products under the name of a corporation. The first restaurants in the Kentucky Fried Chicken chain were opened. In the 1950s, Sanders created the Colonel Sanders persona (he had been made an honorary colonel by the governor of Kentucky in the 1930s) and continued to appear in advertisements for the restaurant chain long after he sold the business in 1964.

LORETTA LYNN
SINGER
BORN: *April 14, 1935, Butcher Holler*

Loretta Webb grew up in a log cabin in rural Johnson County. When she was thirteen she married Oliver "Doolittle" Lynn and moved with him to Washington State, where she had four children by the time she was eighteen. In 1960, she recorded "I'm a Honky Tonk Girl," and her husband mailed copies of the record to radio stations around the country. The song became a hit, and she signed with Decca records.

Her many awards have included three Country Music Association (CMA) awards for Female Vocalist of the Year, CMA Entertainer of the Decade (1980), and a Grammy award. The movie *Coal Miner's Daughter* (1980) is about her life.

MUHAMMAD ALI
BOXER
BORN: *January 17, 1942, Louisville*

Self-proclaimed "The Greatest," Muhammad Ali, who was born Cassius Clay, is considered the quickest heavyweight in boxing history. Ali began taking lessons in boxing from a Louisville policeman when he was twelve. In 1960, he won a gold medal at the Olympics in Rome in the 178-pound (81-kg) division. He won his first world heavyweight championship in 1964, knocking out Sonny Liston. Later that year, when he converted to Islam, he changed his name. Because of his religious beliefs, he refused to serve in the military when he was drafted in 1967. Ali was arrested and stripped of his title, but in 1971 the U.S. Supreme Court ruled that the action had been illegal. He regained the world heavyweight championship in 1974, defeating George Foreman. He lost the crown in 1978 to Leon Spinks, then defeated Spinks later that year to regain it. He held the title until 1980, when he lost to Larry Holmes.

Kentucky
History At-A-Glance

1774
The first permanent non-Native settlement, Fort Harrod, is established.

1775
Daniel Boone establishes Fort Boonesborough.

1778
Present-day Kentucky falls under Virginia's control.

1792
Kentucky becomes the fifteenth state.

1799
The second state constitution is adopted, guaranteeing legality of slavery.

1818
The Jackson Purchase adds 2,000 square miles (5,180 sq km) of land to Kentucky.

1850
The third state constitution is adopted and slavery remains legal.

1862
Confederate forces gain control of Lexington and Frankfort in August. In October, Union forces retake the state.

1865
The federal government imposes martial law after the end of the Civil War.

1880
Kentucky produces one million tons of coal.

1878
The Hatfield-McCoy feud begins.

1891
The fourth state constitution is adopted.

1600   **1700**   **1800**

1492
Christopher Columbus comes to New World.

1607
Capt. John Smith and three ships land on Virginia coast and start first English settlement in New World — Jamestown.

1754–63
French and Indian War.

1773
Boston Tea Party.

1776
Declaration of Independence adopted July 4.

1777
Articles of Confederation adopted by Continental Congress.

1787
U.S. Constitution written.

1812–14
War of 1812.

United States
History At-A-Glance

1941 KENTUCKY DERBY CHURCHILL DOWNS LOUISVILLE

1908
The Sullivan Law calls for state-funded public education in Kentucky for the first time.

1925
Mary Breckenridge establishes the Frontier Nursing Service.

1944
The Kentucky Dam is completed.

1955
Desegregation of Kentucky's public colleges is completed.

1967
Georgia Powers is the first woman and first African American elected to the Kentucky State Senate.

1974
Tornadoes strike the state twenty-six times in nine hours, causing approximately $110 million in damages.

1915–19
With the wartime economy, Kentucky begins to recover from Reconstruction.

1935
Charles W. Anderson becomes the first African-American state legislator since Reconstruction.

1948
Desegregation of Kentucky hospitals and libraries begins.

1966
Kentucky Civil Rights Act is passed.

1970s
Kentucky becomes the nation's top coal producer.

1990
KERA, a groundbreaking education reform bill, is passed by the General Assembly.

1800	1900	2000

1848
Gold discovered in California draws eighty thousand prospectors in the 1849 Gold Rush.

1869
Transcontinental railroad completed.

1929
Stock market crash ushers in Great Depression.

1950–53
U.S. fights in the Korean War.

2000
George W. Bush wins the closest presidential election in history.

1861–65
Civil War.

1917–18
U.S. involvement in World War I.

1941–45
U.S. involvement in World War II.

1964–73
U.S. involvement in Vietnam War.

2001
A terrorist attack in which four hijacked airliners crash into New York City's World Trade Center, the Pentagon, and farmland in western Pennsylvania leaves thousands dead or injured.

▼ Horses parade to the post for the running of the 1941 Kentucky Derby.

PHOTO BY CAUFIELD COPYRIGHTED

Festivals and Fun for All

Check web site for exact date and directions.

Annual Quilt Show, Paducah

The American Quilter's Society's annual show features lectures, merchants, and, of course, quilts.
www.aqsquilt.com/aqsshows.shtml

Battle of Perryville, Perryville

Each October reenactors from the North–South Alliance re-create the famous battle at the Perryville Battlefield State Historic Park.
www.battleofperryville.com

Catch a Rainbow Kids Fishing Derby, Jamestown

In early June, kids and their parents can enjoy a day of fishing together on Lake Cumberland and win prizes, while also learning about wildlife conservation.
www.lakecumberlandvacation.com

Emancipation Celebration, Paducah

Every August at the W. C. Young Community Center, people gather to celebrate the 1863 emancipation of African-American slaves. The event includes a parade, memorial service, picnic, concert, and fashion show.
www.paducahky.com/festivals.html

Festival of the Bluegrass, Lexington

Enjoy bluegrass music in the Bluegrass State. This four-day event takes place at the Kentucky Horse Park.
www.kyfestival.com

Great American Brass Band Festival, Danville

Three days of brass band music and a picnic headline this festival.
www.gabbf.com

Humana Festival of New American Plays, Louisville

The Actors Theatre of Louisville presents one of the top venues in the nation for new theatrical works.
www.actorstheatre.org

International Bar-B-Q Festival, Owensboro

During the second weekend in May, the waterfront in this town on the banks of the Ohio River is turned over to teams of barbecue chefs, who compete for honors in the categories of chicken, mutton, and burgoo, as well as "Best Overall Bar-B-Q team." The festival also includes live music and local arts and crafts.
www.bbqfest.com

Kentucky Celtic Festival and Highland Games, Hopkinsville

This celebration of Celtic heritage features a demonstration of traditional Scottish athletics.
www.kiltedkinsmen.tripod.com

◄ Entrants prepare for the Kentucky Derby Festival Balloon Race.

community and a living museum dedicated to the unique lifestyle of Shakers in America. Visitors can see demonstrations of Shaker handicrafts, such as spinning and weaving, or go for a ride on a Civil War-era riverboat. www.shakervillageky.org

Kentucky Derby Festival, Louisville

The biggest horse race in the nation demands the biggest festival — including festival princesses, a hot-air balloon race, and much more.
www.kdf.org

Kentucky Shakespeare Festival, Louisville

Performances of Shakespeare's works are produced in Louisville's Central Park.
www.kyshakes.org

Pioneer Days Festival, Harrodsburg

Concerts, fireworks, and historical demonstrations are the highlights of this annual event.
www.pioneerdays.org

The Poppy Mountain Bluegrass Festival, Morehead

This sixteen-day festival of bluegrass music takes place at Poppy Mountain. When you're not listening to the music, you can fish, hike, or ride horseback.
www.poppymountainbluegrass.com

Shaker Village of Pleasant Hill, Harrodsburg

Pleasant Hill is a re-creation of a Shaker

Southern Kentucky Festival of Books, Bowling Green

This festival is devoted to increasing literacy and features writing workshops, performances, book dealers, children's events, and more than 150 authors.
www.sokybookfest.org

W. C. Handy Blues and Barbecue Festival, Henderson

The festival of music named for the father of the blues also features a Mardi Gras party.
www.handyblues.org

Wildflower Weekend, Slade

During the first weekend in May, experts lead walks in the woods to look at spring's first flowers.
www.state.ky.us/agencies/parks/i75frames/natbridg-body.htm

The World's Championship Horse Show, Louisville

Kentucky is famous for horses and not just thoroughbreds. This horse show is for saddlebreds, the only horse breed to have originated within the state. It is held during the Kentucky State Fair.
www.kystatefair.org/wcns/home.htm

Books

Appelt, Kathi, and Jeanne Cannella Schmitzer. *Down Cut Shin Creek: The Packhorse Librarians of Kentucky.* New York: HarperCollins, 2001. During the Great Depression and in the years following, men and women served as "librarians on horseback," bringing books and other reading materials to Kentucky's rural poor.

Capek, Michael. *A Personal Tour of a Shaker Village.* Minneapolis: Lerner Publications, 2001. A look at life in the Shaker village of Pleasant Hill during the mid-1800s.

Kozar, Richard. *Daniel Boone and the Exploration of the Frontier.* Broomall, PA: Chelsea House, 1999. A biography of Daniel Boone for young readers.

Meltzer, Milton. *Underground Man.* New York: Harcourt, 1990. The fact-based story of a white abolitionist who helped slaves escape Kentucky via the Underground Railroad.

Wells, Rosemary. *Mary on Horseback: Three Mountain Stories.* New York: Penguin/Putnam, 2000. Three stories show life in rural Kentucky in the early 1900s and the profound effect of Mary Breckenridge's Frontier Nursing Service.

Web Sites

▶ Official state web site
www.state.ky.us

▶ Frankfort/Franklin County Tourist and Convention Commission
www.visitfrankfort.com

▶ Kentucky Historical Society
www.kyhistory.org

▶ Mammoth Cave National Park
www.nps.gov/maca/index.htm